Stay on
TARGET

A Meal Planner for Healthy Weight Loss

Copyright 2016

All Rights reserved. No part of this book may be reproduced or used in any way or formor by any means whether electronic or mechanical, this means that you cannot recordor photocopy any material ideas or tips that are provided in this book.

ZERO CALORIE FOODS

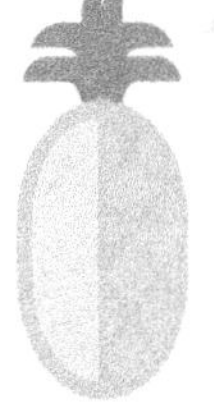

pineapple

apricot

lemon

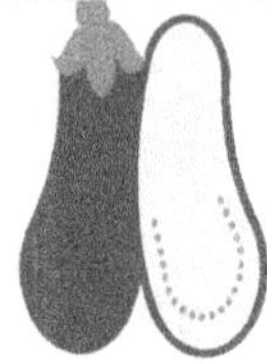

aubergine

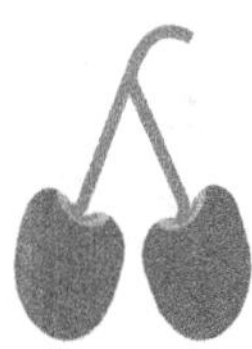

blueberries

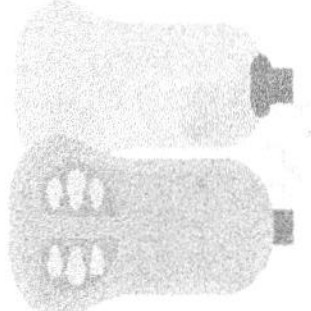

butternut squash

cauliflower

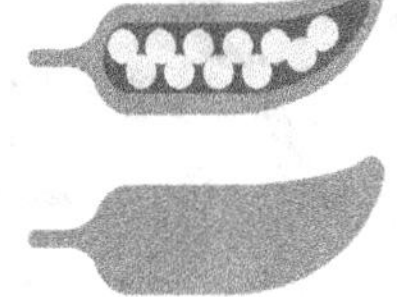

chilli peppers

cranberries

onion

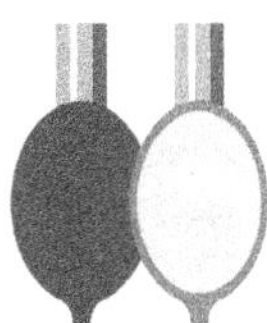

beetroot

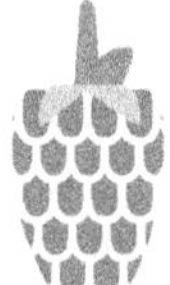

raspberries

watermelon

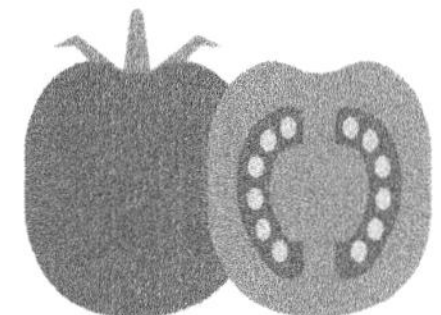

tomato

apple

lettuce

lime

mango

turnip

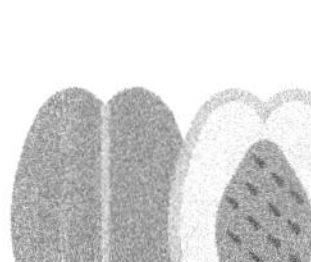

peach

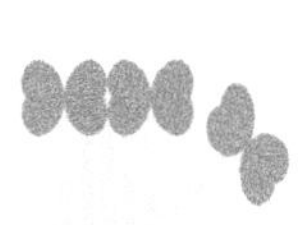

cress

endive

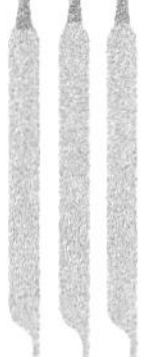

green bean

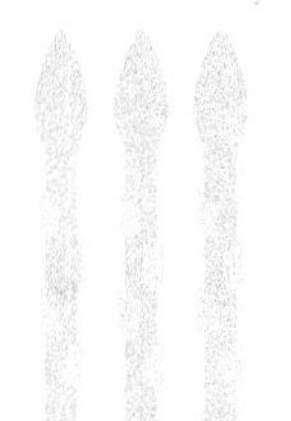

asparagus

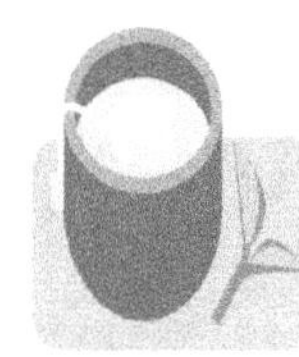

green tea

How many calories ?

30	138	216	249
266	305	311	312
318	321	406	452

MEAL PLANNER

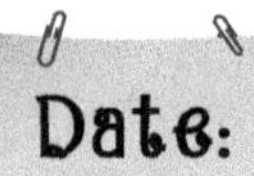

Date:

	DESCRIPTION	QTY	PROTEINS	VEGGIES	FRUITS & NUTS	FATS
BREAK FAST						
TIME						
TOTAL						

	DESCRIPTION	QTY	PROTEINS	VEGGIES	FRUITS & NUTS	FATS
LUNCH						
TIME						
TOTAL						

	DESCRIPTION	QTY	PROTEINS	VEGGIES	FRUITS & NUTS	FATS
DINNER						
TIME						
TOTAL						

	DESCRIPTION	QTY	PROTEINS	VEGGIES	FRUITS & NUTS	FATS
SNACK						
TIME						
TOTAL						

Meal Planner

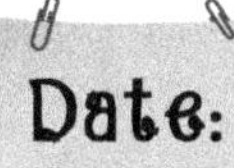

Date:

	DESCRIPTION	QTY	PROTEINS	VEGGIES	FRUITS & NUTS	FATS
BREAK FAST						
TIME						
TOTAL						

	DESCRIPTION	QTY	PROTEINS	VEGGIES	FRUITS & NUTS	FATS
LUNCH						
TIME						
TOTAL						

	DESCRIPTION	QTY	PROTEINS	VEGGIES	FRUITS & NUTS	FATS
DINNER						
TIME						
TOTAL						

	DESCRIPTION	QTY	PROTEINS	VEGGIES	FRUITS & NUTS	FATS
SNACK						
TIME						
TOTAL						

MEAL PLANNER

Date:

BREAK FAST

TIME

DESCRIPTION	QTY	PROTEINS	VEGGIES	FRUITS & NUTS	FATS
TOTAL					

LUNCH

TIME

DESCRIPTION	QTY	PROTEINS	VEGGIES	FRUITS & NUTS	FATS
TOTAL					

DINNER

TIME

DESCRIPTION	QTY	PROTEINS	VEGGIES	FRUITS & NUTS	FATS
TOTAL					

SNACK

TIME

DESCRIPTION	QTY	PROTEINS	VEGGIES	FRUITS & NUTS	FATS
TOTAL					

MEAL PLANNER

Date:

BREAK FAST

TIME

DESCRIPTION	QTY	PROTEINS	VEGGIES	FRUITS & NUTS	FATS
TOTAL					

LUNCH

TIME

DESCRIPTION	QTY	PROTEINS	VEGGIES	FRUITS & NUTS	FATS
TOTAL					

DINNER

TIME

DESCRIPTION	QTY	PROTEINS	VEGGIES	FRUITS & NUTS	FATS
TOTAL					

SNACK

TIME

DESCRIPTION	QTY	PROTEINS	VEGGIES	FRUITS & NUTS	FATS
TOTAL					

MEAL PLANNER

BREAK FAST

TIME

	DESCRIPTION	QTY	PROTEINS	VEGGIES	FRUITS & NUTS	FATS
TOTAL						

LUNCH

TIME

	DESCRIPTION	QTY	PROTEINS	VEGGIES	FRUITS & NUTS	FATS
TOTAL						

DINNER

TIME

	DESCRIPTION	QTY	PROTEINS	VEGGIES	FRUITS & NUTS	FATS
TOTAL						

SNACK

TIME

	DESCRIPTION	QTY	PROTEINS	VEGGIES	FRUITS & NUTS	FATS
TOTAL						

Meal Planner

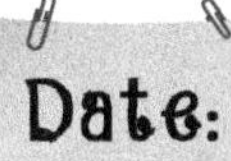

Date:

BREAK FAST

TIME

DESCRIPTION	QTY	PROTEINS	VEGGIES	FRUITS & NUTS	FATS
TOTAL					

LUNCH

TIME

DESCRIPTION	QTY	PROTEINS	VEGGIES	FRUITS & NUTS	FATS
TOTAL					

DINNER

TIME

DESCRIPTION	QTY	PROTEINS	VEGGIES	FRUITS & NUTS	FATS
TOTAL					

SNACK

TIME

DESCRIPTION	QTY	PROTEINS	VEGGIES	FRUITS & NUTS	FATS
TOTAL					

MEAL PLANNER

BREAK FAST

TIME

TOTAL

DESCRIPTION	QTY	PROTEINS	VEGGIES	FRUITS & NUTS	FATS

LUNCH

TIME

TOTAL

DESCRIPTION	QTY	PROTEINS	VEGGIES	FRUITS & NUTS	FATS

DINNER

TIME

TOTAL

DESCRIPTION	QTY	PROTEINS	VEGGIES	FRUITS & NUTS	FATS

SNACK

TIME

TOTAL

DESCRIPTION	QTY	PROTEINS	VEGGIES	FRUITS & NUTS	FATS

MeaL PLanneR

Date:

BREAK FAST

TIME

	DESCRIPTION	QTY	PROTEINS	VEGGIES	FRUITS & NUTS	FATS
TOTAL						

LUNCH

TIME

	DESCRIPTION	QTY	PROTEINS	VEGGIES	FRUITS & NUTS	FATS
TOTAL						

DINNER

TIME

	DESCRIPTION	QTY	PROTEINS	VEGGIES	FRUITS & NUTS	FATS
TOTAL						

SNACK

TIME

	DESCRIPTION	QTY	PROTEINS	VEGGIES	FRUITS & NUTS	FATS
TOTAL						

MEAL PLANNER

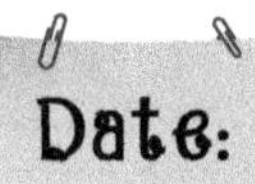

Date:

BREAK FAST	DESCRIPTION	QTY	PROTEINS	VEGGIES	FRUITS & NUTS	FATS
TIME						
TOTAL						

LUNCH	DESCRIPTION	QTY	PROTEINS	VEGGIES	FRUITS & NUTS	FATS
TIME						
TOTAL						

DINNER	DESCRIPTION	QTY	PROTEINS	VEGGIES	FRUITS & NUTS	FATS
TIME						
TOTAL						

SNACK	DESCRIPTION	QTY	PROTEINS	VEGGIES	FRUITS & NUTS	FATS
TIME						
TOTAL						

MEAL PLANNER

	DESCRIPTION	QTY	PROTEINS	VEGGIES	FRUITS & NUTS	FATS
BREAK FAST						
TIME						
TOTAL						

	DESCRIPTION	QTY	PROTEINS	VEGGIES	FRUITS & NUTS	FATS
LUNCH						
TIME						
TOTAL						

	DESCRIPTION	QTY	PROTEINS	VEGGIES	FRUITS & NUTS	FATS
DINNER						
TIME						
TOTAL						

	DESCRIPTION	QTY	PROTEINS	VEGGIES	FRUITS & NUTS	FATS
SNACK						
TIME						
TOTAL						

meal planner

Date:

	DESCRIPTION	QTY	PROTEINS	VEGGIES	FRUITS & NUTS	FATS
BREAK FAST						
TIME						
TOTAL						

	DESCRIPTION	QTY	PROTEINS	VEGGIES	FRUITS & NUTS	FATS
LUNCH						
TIME						
TOTAL						

	DESCRIPTION	QTY	PROTEINS	VEGGIES	FRUITS & NUTS	FATS
DINNER						
TIME						
TOTAL						

	DESCRIPTION	QTY	PROTEINS	VEGGIES	FRUITS & NUTS	FATS
SNACK						
TIME						
TOTAL						

meal planner

Date:

BREAK FAST

TIME

DESCRIPTION	QTY	PROTEINS	VEGGIES	FRUITS & NUTS	FATS
TOTAL					

LUNCH

TIME

DESCRIPTION	QTY	PROTEINS	VEGGIES	FRUITS & NUTS	FATS
TOTAL					

DINNER

TIME

DESCRIPTION	QTY	PROTEINS	VEGGIES	FRUITS & NUTS	FATS
TOTAL					

SNACK

TIME

DESCRIPTION	QTY	PROTEINS	VEGGIES	FRUITS & NUTS	FATS
TOTAL					

MEAL PLANNER

Date:

	DESCRIPTION	QTY	PROTEINS	VEGGIES	FRUITS & NUTS	FATS
BREAK FAST						
TIME						
TOTAL						

	DESCRIPTION	QTY	PROTEINS	VEGGIES	FRUITS & NUTS	FATS
LUNCH						
TIME						
TOTAL						

	DESCRIPTION	QTY	PROTEINS	VEGGIES	FRUITS & NUTS	FATS
DINNER						
TIME						
TOTAL						

	DESCRIPTION	QTY	PROTEINS	VEGGIES	FRUITS & NUTS	FATS
SNACK						
TIME						
TOTAL						

MEAL PLANNER

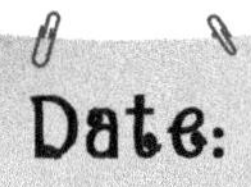

Date:

BREAK FAST

TIME

DESCRIPTION	QTY	PROTEINS	VEGGIES	FRUITS & NUTS	FATS
TOTAL					

LUNCH

TIME

DESCRIPTION	QTY	PROTEINS	VEGGIES	FRUITS & NUTS	FATS
TOTAL					

DINNER

TIME

DESCRIPTION	QTY	PROTEINS	VEGGIES	FRUITS & NUTS	FATS
TOTAL					

SNACK

TIME

DESCRIPTION	QTY	PROTEINS	VEGGIES	FRUITS & NUTS	FATS
TOTAL					

MEAL PLANNER

Date:

	DESCRIPTION	QTY	PROTEINS	VEGGIES	FRUITS & NUTS	FATS
BREAK FAST TIME						
TOTAL						

	DESCRIPTION	QTY	PROTEINS	VEGGIES	FRUITS & NUTS	FATS
LUNCH TIME						
TOTAL						

	DESCRIPTION	QTY	PROTEINS	VEGGIES	FRUITS & NUTS	FATS
DINNER TIME						
TOTAL						

	DESCRIPTION	QTY	PROTEINS	VEGGIES	FRUITS & NUTS	FATS
SNACK TIME						
TOTAL						

meal planner

Date:

BREAK FAST

TIME

TOTAL

DESCRIPTION	QTY	PROTEINS	VEGGIES	FRUITS & NUTS	FATS

LUNCH

TIME

TOTAL

DESCRIPTION	QTY	PROTEINS	VEGGIES	FRUITS & NUTS	FATS

DINNER

TIME

TOTAL

DESCRIPTION	QTY	PROTEINS	VEGGIES	FRUITS & NUTS	FATS

SNACK

TIME

TOTAL

DESCRIPTION	QTY	PROTEINS	VEGGIES	FRUITS & NUTS	FATS

meal planner

Date:

	DESCRIPTION	QTY	PROTEINS	VEGGIES	FRUITS & NUTS	FATS
BREAK FAST						
TIME						
TOTAL						

	DESCRIPTION	QTY	PROTEINS	VEGGIES	FRUITS & NUTS	FATS
LUNCH						
TIME						
TOTAL						

	DESCRIPTION	QTY	PROTEINS	VEGGIES	FRUITS & NUTS	FATS
DINNER						
TIME						
TOTAL						

	DESCRIPTION	QTY	PROTEINS	VEGGIES	FRUITS & NUTS	FATS
SNACK						
TIME						
TOTAL						

MEAL PLANNER

Date:

BREAK FAST

TIME

DESCRIPTION	QTY	PROTEINS	VEGGIES	FRUITS & NUTS	FATS
TOTAL					

LUNCH

TIME

DESCRIPTION	QTY	PROTEINS	VEGGIES	FRUITS & NUTS	FATS
TOTAL					

DINNER

TIME

DESCRIPTION	QTY	PROTEINS	VEGGIES	FRUITS & NUTS	FATS
TOTAL					

SNACK

TIME

DESCRIPTION	QTY	PROTEINS	VEGGIES	FRUITS & NUTS	FATS
TOTAL					

MEAL PLANNER

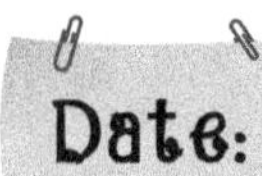

Date:

BREAK FAST

TIME

DESCRIPTION	QTY	PROTEINS	VEGGIES	FRUITS & NUTS	FATS
TOTAL					

LUNCH

TIME

DESCRIPTION	QTY	PROTEINS	VEGGIES	FRUITS & NUTS	FATS
TOTAL					

DINNER

TIME

DESCRIPTION	QTY	PROTEINS	VEGGIES	FRUITS & NUTS	FATS
TOTAL					

SNACK

TIME

DESCRIPTION	QTY	PROTEINS	VEGGIES	FRUITS & NUTS	FATS
TOTAL					

Meal Planner

Date:

	DESCRIPTION	QTY	PROTEINS	VEGGIES	FRUITS & NUTS	FATS
BREAK FAST						
TIME						
TOTAL						

	DESCRIPTION	QTY	PROTEINS	VEGGIES	FRUITS & NUTS	FATS
LUNCH						
TIME						
TOTAL						

	DESCRIPTION	QTY	PROTEINS	VEGGIES	FRUITS & NUTS	FATS
DINNER						
TIME						
TOTAL						

	DESCRIPTION	QTY	PROTEINS	VEGGIES	FRUITS & NUTS	FATS
SNACK						
TIME						
TOTAL						

Meal Planner

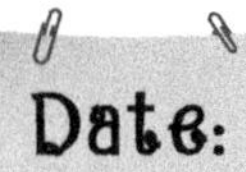

Date:

BREAK FAST

TIME

DESCRIPTION	QTY	PROTEINS	VEGGIES	FRUITS & NUTS	FATS
TOTAL					

LUNCH

TIME

DESCRIPTION	QTY	PROTEINS	VEGGIES	FRUITS & NUTS	FATS
TOTAL					

DINNER

TIME

DESCRIPTION	QTY	PROTEINS	VEGGIES	FRUITS & NUTS	FATS
TOTAL					

SNACK

TIME

DESCRIPTION	QTY	PROTEINS	VEGGIES	FRUITS & NUTS	FATS
TOTAL					

meal planner

Date:

BREAK FAST

TIME

DESCRIPTION	QTY	PROTEINS	VEGGIES	FRUITS & NUTS	FATS
TOTAL					

LUNCH

TIME

DESCRIPTION	QTY	PROTEINS	VEGGIES	FRUITS & NUTS	FATS
TOTAL					

DINNER

TIME

DESCRIPTION	QTY	PROTEINS	VEGGIES	FRUITS & NUTS	FATS
TOTAL					

SNACK

TIME

DESCRIPTION	QTY	PROTEINS	VEGGIES	FRUITS & NUTS	FATS
TOTAL					

MEAL PLANNER

BREAK FAST

TIME

DESCRIPTION	QTY	PROTEINS	VEGGIES	FRUITS & NUTS	FATS
TOTAL					

LUNCH

TIME

DESCRIPTION	QTY	PROTEINS	VEGGIES	FRUITS & NUTS	FATS
TOTAL					

DINNER

TIME

DESCRIPTION	QTY	PROTEINS	VEGGIES	FRUITS & NUTS	FATS
TOTAL					

SNACK

TIME

DESCRIPTION	QTY	PROTEINS	VEGGIES	FRUITS & NUTS	FATS
TOTAL					

MEAL PLANNER

BREAK FAST

TIME

DESCRIPTION	QTY	PROTEINS	VEGGIES	FRUITS & NUTS	FATS
TOTAL					

LUNCH

TIME

DESCRIPTION	QTY	PROTEINS	VEGGIES	FRUITS & NUTS	FATS
TOTAL					

DINNER

TIME

DESCRIPTION	QTY	PROTEINS	VEGGIES	FRUITS & NUTS	FATS
TOTAL					

SNACK

TIME

DESCRIPTION	QTY	PROTEINS	VEGGIES	FRUITS & NUTS	FATS
TOTAL					

MEAL PLANNER

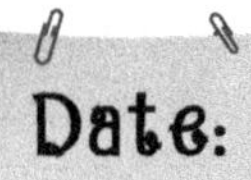

Date:

BREAK FAST	DESCRIPTION	QTY	PROTEINS	VEGGIES	FRUITS & NUTS	FATS
TIME						
TOTAL						

LUNCH	DESCRIPTION	QTY	PROTEINS	VEGGIES	FRUITS & NUTS	FATS
TIME						
TOTAL						

DINNER	DESCRIPTION	QTY	PROTEINS	VEGGIES	FRUITS & NUTS	FATS
TIME						
TOTAL						

SNACK	DESCRIPTION	QTY	PROTEINS	VEGGIES	FRUITS & NUTS	FATS
TIME						
TOTAL						

MEAL PLANNER

Date:

BREAK FAST

TIME

DESCRIPTION	QTY	PROTEINS	VEGGIES	FRUITS & NUTS	FATS
TOTAL					

LUNCH

TIME

DESCRIPTION	QTY	PROTEINS	VEGGIES	FRUITS & NUTS	FATS
TOTAL					

DINNER

TIME

DESCRIPTION	QTY	PROTEINS	VEGGIES	FRUITS & NUTS	FATS
TOTAL					

SNACK

TIME

DESCRIPTION	QTY	PROTEINS	VEGGIES	FRUITS & NUTS	FATS
TOTAL					

Meal Planner

Date:

	DESCRIPTION	QTY	PROTEINS	VEGGIES	FRUITS & NUTS	FATS
BREAK FAST						
TIME						
TOTAL						

	DESCRIPTION	QTY	PROTEINS	VEGGIES	FRUITS & NUTS	FATS
LUNCH						
TIME						
TOTAL						

	DESCRIPTION	QTY	PROTEINS	VEGGIES	FRUITS & NUTS	FATS
DINNER						
TIME						
TOTAL						

	DESCRIPTION	QTY	PROTEINS	VEGGIES	FRUITS & NUTS	FATS
SNACK						
TIME						
TOTAL						

MEAL PLANNER

Date:

BREAK FAST

TIME

DESCRIPTION	QTY	PROTEINS	VEGGIES	FRUITS & NUTS	FATS
TOTAL					

LUNCH

TIME

DESCRIPTION	QTY	PROTEINS	VEGGIES	FRUITS & NUTS	FATS
TOTAL					

DINNER

TIME

DESCRIPTION	QTY	PROTEINS	VEGGIES	FRUITS & NUTS	FATS
TOTAL					

SNACK

TIME

DESCRIPTION	QTY	PROTEINS	VEGGIES	FRUITS & NUTS	FATS
TOTAL					

Meal Planner

Date:

	DESCRIPTION	QTY	PROTEINS	VEGGIES	FRUITS & NUTS	FATS
BREAK FAST						
TIME						
TOTAL						

	DESCRIPTION	QTY	PROTEINS	VEGGIES	FRUITS & NUTS	FATS
LUNCH						
TIME						
TOTAL						

	DESCRIPTION	QTY	PROTEINS	VEGGIES	FRUITS & NUTS	FATS
DINNER						
TIME						
TOTAL						

	DESCRIPTION	QTY	PROTEINS	VEGGIES	FRUITS & NUTS	FATS
SNACK						
TIME						
TOTAL						

meal planner

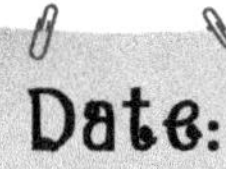

Date:

BREAKFAST

DESCRIPTION	QTY	PROTEINS	VEGGIES	FRUITS & NUTS	FATS
TOTAL					

TIME

LUNCH

DESCRIPTION	QTY	PROTEINS	VEGGIES	FRUITS & NUTS	FATS
TOTAL					

TIME

DINNER

DESCRIPTION	QTY	PROTEINS	VEGGIES	FRUITS & NUTS	FATS
TOTAL					

TIME

SNACK

DESCRIPTION	QTY	PROTEINS	VEGGIES	FRUITS & NUTS	FATS
TOTAL					

TIME

MEAL PLANNER

Date:

BREAK FAST

TIME

DESCRIPTION	QTY	PROTEINS	VEGGIES	FRUITS & NUTS	FATS
TOTAL					

LUNCH

TIME

DESCRIPTION	QTY	PROTEINS	VEGGIES	FRUITS & NUTS	FATS
TOTAL					

DINNER

TIME

DESCRIPTION	QTY	PROTEINS	VEGGIES	FRUITS & NUTS	FATS
TOTAL					

SNACK

TIME

DESCRIPTION	QTY	PROTEINS	VEGGIES	FRUITS & NUTS	FATS
TOTAL					

Meal Planner

Date:

BREAK FAST

DESCRIPTION	QTY	PROTEINS	VEGGIES	FRUITS & NUTS	FATS
TOTAL					

TIME

LUNCH

DESCRIPTION	QTY	PROTEINS	VEGGIES	FRUITS & NUTS	FATS
TOTAL					

TIME

DINNER

DESCRIPTION	QTY	PROTEINS	VEGGIES	FRUITS & NUTS	FATS
TOTAL					

TIME

SNACK

DESCRIPTION	QTY	PROTEINS	VEGGIES	FRUITS & NUTS	FATS
TOTAL					

TIME

meal planner

BREAK FAST

TIME

DESCRIPTION	QTY	PROTEINS	VEGGIES	FRUITS & NUTS	FATS
TOTAL					

LUNCH

TIME

DESCRIPTION	QTY	PROTEINS	VEGGIES	FRUITS & NUTS	FATS
TOTAL					

DINNER

TIME

DESCRIPTION	QTY	PROTEINS	VEGGIES	FRUITS & NUTS	FATS
TOTAL					

SNACK

TIME

DESCRIPTION	QTY	PROTEINS	VEGGIES	FRUITS & NUTS	FATS
TOTAL					

MEAL PLANNER

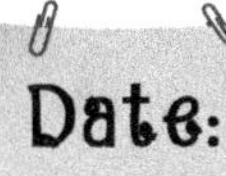

Date:

BREAK FAST

TIME

DESCRIPTION	QTY	PROTEINS	VEGGIES	FRUITS & NUTS	FATS
TOTAL					

LUNCH

TIME

DESCRIPTION	QTY	PROTEINS	VEGGIES	FRUITS & NUTS	FATS
TOTAL					

DINNER

TIME

DESCRIPTION	QTY	PROTEINS	VEGGIES	FRUITS & NUTS	FATS
TOTAL					

SNACK

TIME

DESCRIPTION	QTY	PROTEINS	VEGGIES	FRUITS & NUTS	FATS
TOTAL					

MEAL PLANNER

Date:

BREAK FAST

TIME

DESCRIPTION	QTY	PROTEINS	VEGGIES	FRUITS & NUTS	FATS
TOTAL					

LUNCH

TIME

DESCRIPTION	QTY	PROTEINS	VEGGIES	FRUITS & NUTS	FATS
TOTAL					

DINNER

TIME

DESCRIPTION	QTY	PROTEINS	VEGGIES	FRUITS & NUTS	FATS
TOTAL					

SNACK

TIME

DESCRIPTION	QTY	PROTEINS	VEGGIES	FRUITS & NUTS	FATS
TOTAL					

meal planner

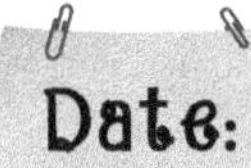

Date:

BREAK FAST

TIME

DESCRIPTION	QTY	PROTEINS	VEGGIES	FRUITS & NUTS	FATS
TOTAL					

LUNCH

TIME

DESCRIPTION	QTY	PROTEINS	VEGGIES	FRUITS & NUTS	FATS
TOTAL					

DINNER

TIME

DESCRIPTION	QTY	PROTEINS	VEGGIES	FRUITS & NUTS	FATS
TOTAL					

SNACK

TIME

DESCRIPTION	QTY	PROTEINS	VEGGIES	FRUITS & NUTS	FATS
TOTAL					

meal Planner

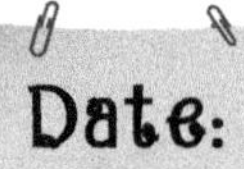

Date:

	DESCRIPTION	QTY	PROTEINS	VEGGIES	FRUITS & NUTS	FATS
BREAK FAST						
TIME ⬭						
TOTAL						

	DESCRIPTION	QTY	PROTEINS	VEGGIES	FRUITS & NUTS	FATS
LUNCH						
TIME ⬭						
TOTAL						

	DESCRIPTION	QTY	PROTEINS	VEGGIES	FRUITS & NUTS	FATS
DINNER						
TIME ⬭						
TOTAL						

	DESCRIPTION	QTY	PROTEINS	VEGGIES	FRUITS & NUTS	FATS
SNACK						
TIME ⬭						
TOTAL						

meal Planner

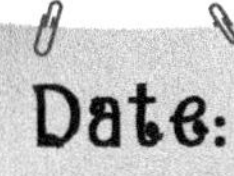

Date:

BREAK FAST

TIME

TOTAL

DESCRIPTION	QTY	PROTEINS	VEGGIES	FRUITS & NUTS	FATS

LUNCH

TIME

TOTAL

DESCRIPTION	QTY	PROTEINS	VEGGIES	FRUITS & NUTS	FATS

DINNER

TIME

TOTAL

DESCRIPTION	QTY	PROTEINS	VEGGIES	FRUITS & NUTS	FATS

SNACK

TIME

TOTAL

DESCRIPTION	QTY	PROTEINS	VEGGIES	FRUITS & NUTS	FATS

meal Planner

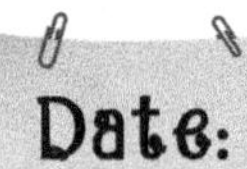

Date:

	DESCRIPTION	QTY	PROTEINS	VEGGIES	FRUITS & NUTS	FATS
BREAK FAST TIME						
TOTAL						

	DESCRIPTION	QTY	PROTEINS	VEGGIES	FRUITS & NUTS	FATS
LUNCH TIME						
TOTAL						

	DESCRIPTION	QTY	PROTEINS	VEGGIES	FRUITS & NUTS	FATS
DINNER TIME						
TOTAL						

	DESCRIPTION	QTY	PROTEINS	VEGGIES	FRUITS & NUTS	FATS
SNACK TIME						
TOTAL						

meal Planner

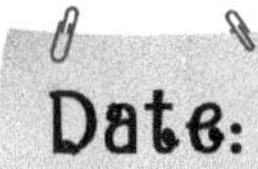

Date:

BREAK FAST

TIME

DESCRIPTION	QTY	PROTEINS	VEGGIES	FRUITS & NUTS	FATS
TOTAL					

LUNCH

TIME

DESCRIPTION	QTY	PROTEINS	VEGGIES	FRUITS & NUTS	FATS
TOTAL					

DINNER

TIME

DESCRIPTION	QTY	PROTEINS	VEGGIES	FRUITS & NUTS	FATS
TOTAL					

SNACK

TIME

DESCRIPTION	QTY	PROTEINS	VEGGIES	FRUITS & NUTS	FATS
TOTAL					

Meal Planner

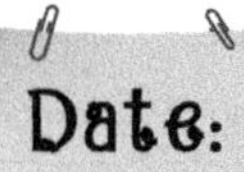

Date:

BREAK FAST	DESCRIPTION	QTY	PROTEINS	VEGGIES	FRUITS & NUTS	FATS
TIME						
TOTAL						

LUNCH	DESCRIPTION	QTY	PROTEINS	VEGGIES	FRUITS & NUTS	FATS
TIME						
TOTAL						

DINNER	DESCRIPTION	QTY	PROTEINS	VEGGIES	FRUITS & NUTS	FATS
TIME						
TOTAL						

SNACK	DESCRIPTION	QTY	PROTEINS	VEGGIES	FRUITS & NUTS	FATS
TIME						
TOTAL						

meal planner

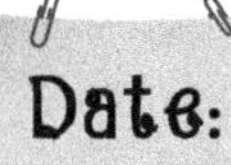 Date:

BREAK FAST

TIME

DESCRIPTION	QTY	PROTEINS	VEGGIES	FRUITS & NUTS	FATS
TOTAL					

LUNCH

TIME

DESCRIPTION	QTY	PROTEINS	VEGGIES	FRUITS & NUTS	FATS
TOTAL					

DINNER

TIME

DESCRIPTION	QTY	PROTEINS	VEGGIES	FRUITS & NUTS	FATS
TOTAL					

SNACK

TIME

DESCRIPTION	QTY	PROTEINS	VEGGIES	FRUITS & NUTS	FATS
TOTAL					

MEAL PLANNER

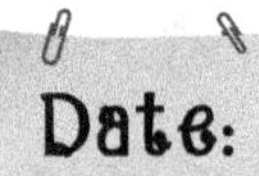

Date:

	DESCRIPTION	QTY	PROTEINS	VEGGIES	FRUITS & NUTS	FATS
BREAK FAST						
TIME						
TOTAL						

	DESCRIPTION	QTY	PROTEINS	VEGGIES	FRUITS & NUTS	FATS
LUNCH						
TIME						
TOTAL						

	DESCRIPTION	QTY	PROTEINS	VEGGIES	FRUITS & NUTS	FATS
DINNER						
TIME						
TOTAL						

	DESCRIPTION	QTY	PROTEINS	VEGGIES	FRUITS & NUTS	FATS
SNACK						
TIME						
TOTAL						

MEAL PLANNER

Date:

BREAK FAST

TIME

DESCRIPTION	QTY	PROTEINS	VEGGIES	FRUITS & NUTS	FATS
TOTAL					

LUNCH

TIME

DESCRIPTION	QTY	PROTEINS	VEGGIES	FRUITS & NUTS	FATS
TOTAL					

DINNER

TIME

DESCRIPTION	QTY	PROTEINS	VEGGIES	FRUITS & NUTS	FATS
TOTAL					

SNACK

TIME

DESCRIPTION	QTY	PROTEINS	VEGGIES	FRUITS & NUTS	FATS
TOTAL					

MEAL PLANNER

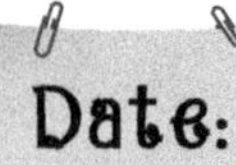

Date:

BREAK FAST

TIME

DESCRIPTION	QTY	PROTEINS	VEGGIES	FRUITS & NUTS	FATS
TOTAL					

LUNCH

TIME

DESCRIPTION	QTY	PROTEINS	VEGGIES	FRUITS & NUTS	FATS
TOTAL					

DINNER

TIME

DESCRIPTION	QTY	PROTEINS	VEGGIES	FRUITS & NUTS	FATS
TOTAL					

SNACK

TIME

DESCRIPTION	QTY	PROTEINS	VEGGIES	FRUITS & NUTS	FATS
TOTAL					

meal planner

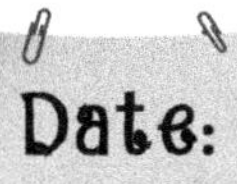

BREAK FAST

TIME

DESCRIPTION	QTY	PROTEINS	VEGGIES	FRUITS & NUTS	FATS
TOTAL					

LUNCH

TIME

DESCRIPTION	QTY	PROTEINS	VEGGIES	FRUITS & NUTS	FATS
TOTAL					

DINNER

TIME

DESCRIPTION	QTY	PROTEINS	VEGGIES	FRUITS & NUTS	FATS
TOTAL					

SNACK

TIME

DESCRIPTION	QTY	PROTEINS	VEGGIES	FRUITS & NUTS	FATS
TOTAL					

MEAL PLANNER

BREAK FAST

TIME

DESCRIPTION	QTY	PROTEINS	VEGGIES	FRUITS & NUTS	FATS
TOTAL					

LUNCH

TIME

DESCRIPTION	QTY	PROTEINS	VEGGIES	FRUITS & NUTS	FATS
TOTAL					

DINNER

TIME

DESCRIPTION	QTY	PROTEINS	VEGGIES	FRUITS & NUTS	FATS
TOTAL					

SNACK

TIME

DESCRIPTION	QTY	PROTEINS	VEGGIES	FRUITS & NUTS	FATS
TOTAL					

MEAL PLANNER

Date:

BREAK FAST	DESCRIPTION	QTY	PROTEINS	VEGGIES	FRUITS & NUTS	FATS
TIME						
TOTAL						

LUNCH	DESCRIPTION	QTY	PROTEINS	VEGGIES	FRUITS & NUTS	FATS
TIME						
TOTAL						

DINNER	DESCRIPTION	QTY	PROTEINS	VEGGIES	FRUITS & NUTS	FATS
TIME						
TOTAL						

SNACK	DESCRIPTION	QTY	PROTEINS	VEGGIES	FRUITS & NUTS	FATS
TIME						
TOTAL						

MEAL PLANNER

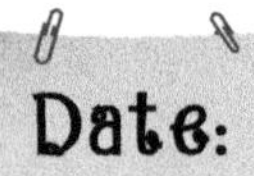

Date:

BREAK FAST

TIME

DESCRIPTION	QTY	PROTEINS	VEGGIES	FRUITS & NUTS	FATS
TOTAL					

LUNCH

TIME

DESCRIPTION	QTY	PROTEINS	VEGGIES	FRUITS & NUTS	FATS
TOTAL					

DINNER

TIME

DESCRIPTION	QTY	PROTEINS	VEGGIES	FRUITS & NUTS	FATS
TOTAL					

SNACK

TIME

DESCRIPTION	QTY	PROTEINS	VEGGIES	FRUITS & NUTS	FATS
TOTAL					

Meal Planner

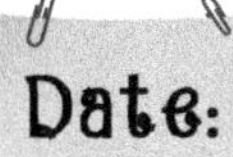

Date:

BREAK FAST

TIME

DESCRIPTION	QTY	PROTEINS	VEGGIES	FRUITS & NUTS	FATS
TOTAL					

LUNCH

TIME

DESCRIPTION	QTY	PROTEINS	VEGGIES	FRUITS & NUTS	FATS
TOTAL					

DINNER

TIME

DESCRIPTION	QTY	PROTEINS	VEGGIES	FRUITS & NUTS	FATS
TOTAL					

SNACK

TIME

DESCRIPTION	QTY	PROTEINS	VEGGIES	FRUITS & NUTS	FATS
TOTAL					

MEAL PLANNER

Date:

BREAK FAST

TIME

DESCRIPTION		QTY	PROTEINS	VEGGIES	FRUITS & NUTS	FATS
TOTAL						

LUNCH

TIME

DESCRIPTION		QTY	PROTEINS	VEGGIES	FRUITS & NUTS	FATS
TOTAL						

DINNER

TIME

DESCRIPTION		QTY	PROTEINS	VEGGIES	FRUITS & NUTS	FATS
TOTAL						

SNACK

TIME

DESCRIPTION		QTY	PROTEINS	VEGGIES	FRUITS & NUTS	FATS
TOTAL						

MEAL PLANNER

BREAK FAST

	DESCRIPTION	QTY	PROTEINS	VEGGIES	FRUITS & NUTS	FATS
TIME						
TOTAL						

LUNCH

	DESCRIPTION	QTY	PROTEINS	VEGGIES	FRUITS & NUTS	FATS
TIME						
TOTAL						

DINNER

	DESCRIPTION	QTY	PROTEINS	VEGGIES	FRUITS & NUTS	FATS
TIME						
TOTAL						

SNACK

	DESCRIPTION	QTY	PROTEINS	VEGGIES	FRUITS & NUTS	FATS
TIME						
TOTAL						

meal planner

Date:

BREAK FAST

TIME

DESCRIPTION	QTY	PROTEINS	VEGGIES	FRUITS & NUTS	FATS
TOTAL					

LUNCH

TIME

DESCRIPTION	QTY	PROTEINS	VEGGIES	FRUITS & NUTS	FATS
TOTAL					

DINNER

TIME

DESCRIPTION	QTY	PROTEINS	VEGGIES	FRUITS & NUTS	FATS
TOTAL					

SNACK

TIME

DESCRIPTION	QTY	PROTEINS	VEGGIES	FRUITS & NUTS	FATS
TOTAL					

MEAL PLANNER

Date:

	DESCRIPTION	QTY	PROTEINS	VEGGIES	FRUITS & NUTS	FATS
BREAK FAST TIME						
TOTAL						

	DESCRIPTION	QTY	PROTEINS	VEGGIES	FRUITS & NUTS	FATS
LUNCH TIME						
TOTAL						

	DESCRIPTION	QTY	PROTEINS	VEGGIES	FRUITS & NUTS	FATS
DINNER TIME						
TOTAL						

	DESCRIPTION	QTY	PROTEINS	VEGGIES	FRUITS & NUTS	FATS
SNACK TIME						
TOTAL						

MEAL PLANNER

Date:

BREAK FAST

TIME

DESCRIPTION	QTY	PROTEINS	VEGGIES	FRUITS & NUTS	FATS
TOTAL					

LUNCH

TIME

DESCRIPTION	QTY	PROTEINS	VEGGIES	FRUITS & NUTS	FATS
TOTAL					

DINNER

TIME

DESCRIPTION	QTY	PROTEINS	VEGGIES	FRUITS & NUTS	FATS
TOTAL					

SNACK

TIME

DESCRIPTION	QTY	PROTEINS	VEGGIES	FRUITS & NUTS	FATS
TOTAL					

MEAL PLANNER

Date:

BREAK FAST

TIME

DESCRIPTION	QTY	PROTEINS	VEGGIES	FRUITS & NUTS	FATS
TOTAL					

LUNCH

TIME

DESCRIPTION	QTY	PROTEINS	VEGGIES	FRUITS & NUTS	FATS
TOTAL					

DINNER

TIME

DESCRIPTION	QTY	PROTEINS	VEGGIES	FRUITS & NUTS	FATS
TOTAL					

SNACK

TIME

DESCRIPTION	QTY	PROTEINS	VEGGIES	FRUITS & NUTS	FATS
TOTAL					

MEAL PLANNER

Date:

BREAK FAST

TIME

DESCRIPTION	QTY	PROTEINS	VEGGIES	FRUITS & NUTS	FATS
TOTAL					

LUNCH

TIME

DESCRIPTION	QTY	PROTEINS	VEGGIES	FRUITS & NUTS	FATS
TOTAL					

DINNER

TIME

DESCRIPTION	QTY	PROTEINS	VEGGIES	FRUITS & NUTS	FATS
TOTAL					

SNACK

TIME

DESCRIPTION	QTY	PROTEINS	VEGGIES	FRUITS & NUTS	FATS
TOTAL					

MEAL PLANNER

Date:

	DESCRIPTION	QTY	PROTEINS	VEGGIES	FRUITS & NUTS	FATS
BREAK FAST						
TIME						
TOTAL						

	DESCRIPTION	QTY	PROTEINS	VEGGIES	FRUITS & NUTS	FATS
LUNCH						
TIME						
TOTAL						

	DESCRIPTION	QTY	PROTEINS	VEGGIES	FRUITS & NUTS	FATS
DINNER						
TIME						
TOTAL						

	DESCRIPTION	QTY	PROTEINS	VEGGIES	FRUITS & NUTS	FATS
SNACK						
TIME						
TOTAL						

mEaL PLaNNER

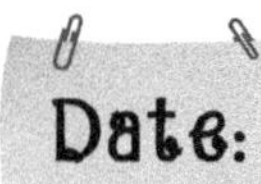

Date:

BREAK FAST

TIME

DESCRIPTION	QTY	PROTEINS	VEGGIES	FRUITS & NUTS	FATS
TOTAL					

LUNCH

TIME

DESCRIPTION	QTY	PROTEINS	VEGGIES	FRUITS & NUTS	FATS
TOTAL					

DINNER

TIME

DESCRIPTION	QTY	PROTEINS	VEGGIES	FRUITS & NUTS	FATS
TOTAL					

SNACK

TIME

DESCRIPTION	QTY	PROTEINS	VEGGIES	FRUITS & NUTS	FATS
TOTAL					

MEAL PLANNER

Date:

BREAK FAST

TIME

DESCRIPTION	QTY	PROTEINS	VEGGIES	FRUITS & NUTS	FATS
TOTAL					

LUNCH

TIME

DESCRIPTION	QTY	PROTEINS	VEGGIES	FRUITS & NUTS	FATS
TOTAL					

DINNER

TIME

DESCRIPTION	QTY	PROTEINS	VEGGIES	FRUITS & NUTS	FATS
TOTAL					

SNACK

TIME

DESCRIPTION	QTY	PROTEINS	VEGGIES	FRUITS & NUTS	FATS
TOTAL					

meal planner

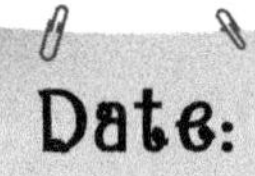

Date:

BREAK FAST	DESCRIPTION	QTY	PROTEINS	VEGGIES	FRUITS & NUTS	FATS
TIME						
TOTAL						

LUNCH	DESCRIPTION	QTY	PROTEINS	VEGGIES	FRUITS & NUTS	FATS
TIME						
TOTAL						

DINNER	DESCRIPTION	QTY	PROTEINS	VEGGIES	FRUITS & NUTS	FATS
TIME						
TOTAL						

SNACK	DESCRIPTION	QTY	PROTEINS	VEGGIES	FRUITS & NUTS	FATS
TIME						
TOTAL						

MEAL PLANNER

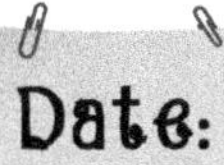

Date:

BREAK FAST

TIME

DESCRIPTION	QTY	PROTEINS	VEGGIES	FRUITS & NUTS	FATS
TOTAL					

LUNCH

TIME

DESCRIPTION	QTY	PROTEINS	VEGGIES	FRUITS & NUTS	FATS
TOTAL					

DINNER

TIME

DESCRIPTION	QTY	PROTEINS	VEGGIES	FRUITS & NUTS	FATS
TOTAL					

SNACK

TIME

DESCRIPTION	QTY	PROTEINS	VEGGIES	FRUITS & NUTS	FATS
TOTAL					

Meal Planner

Date:

BREAK FAST

TIME

DESCRIPTION	QTY	PROTEINS	VEGGIES	FRUITS & NUTS	FATS
TOTAL					

LUNCH

TIME

DESCRIPTION	QTY	PROTEINS	VEGGIES	FRUITS & NUTS	FATS
TOTAL					

DINNER

TIME

DESCRIPTION	QTY	PROTEINS	VEGGIES	FRUITS & NUTS	FATS
TOTAL					

SNACK

TIME

DESCRIPTION	QTY	PROTEINS	VEGGIES	FRUITS & NUTS	FATS
TOTAL					

MEAL PLANNER

Date:

BREAK FAST

TIME

DESCRIPTION	QTY	PROTEINS	VEGGIES	FRUITS & NUTS	FATS
TOTAL					

LUNCH

TIME

DESCRIPTION	QTY	PROTEINS	VEGGIES	FRUITS & NUTS	FATS
TOTAL					

DINNER

TIME

DESCRIPTION	QTY	PROTEINS	VEGGIES	FRUITS & NUTS	FATS
TOTAL					

SNACK

TIME

DESCRIPTION	QTY	PROTEINS	VEGGIES	FRUITS & NUTS	FATS
TOTAL					

MEAL PLANNER

Date:

	DESCRIPTION	QTY	PROTEINS	VEGGIES	FRUITS & NUTS	FATS
BREAK FAST						
TIME						
TOTAL						

	DESCRIPTION	QTY	PROTEINS	VEGGIES	FRUITS & NUTS	FATS
LUNCH						
TIME						
TOTAL						

	DESCRIPTION	QTY	PROTEINS	VEGGIES	FRUITS & NUTS	FATS
DINNER						
TIME						
TOTAL						

	DESCRIPTION	QTY	PROTEINS	VEGGIES	FRUITS & NUTS	FATS
SNACK						
TIME						
TOTAL						

MEAL PLANNER

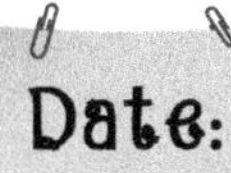

Date:

BREAK FAST

TIME ⬭

DESCRIPTION	QTY	PROTEINS	VEGGIES	FRUITS & NUTS	FATS
TOTAL					

LUNCH

TIME ⬭

DESCRIPTION	QTY	PROTEINS	VEGGIES	FRUITS & NUTS	FATS
TOTAL					

DINNER

TIME ⬭

DESCRIPTION	QTY	PROTEINS	VEGGIES	FRUITS & NUTS	FATS
TOTAL					

SNACK

TIME ⬭

DESCRIPTION	QTY	PROTEINS	VEGGIES	FRUITS & NUTS	FATS
TOTAL					

MEAL PLANNER

Date:

BREAK FAST

TIME

DESCRIPTION	QTY	PROTEINS	VEGGIES	FRUITS & NUTS	FATS
TOTAL					

LUNCH

TIME

DESCRIPTION	QTY	PROTEINS	VEGGIES	FRUITS & NUTS	FATS
TOTAL					

DINNER

TIME

DESCRIPTION	QTY	PROTEINS	VEGGIES	FRUITS & NUTS	FATS
TOTAL					

SNACK

TIME

DESCRIPTION	QTY	PROTEINS	VEGGIES	FRUITS & NUTS	FATS
TOTAL					

MEAL PLANNER

Date:

BREAK FAST	DESCRIPTION	QTY	PROTEINS	VEGGIES	FRUITS & NUTS	FATS
TIME						
TOTAL						

LUNCH	DESCRIPTION	QTY	PROTEINS	VEGGIES	FRUITS & NUTS	FATS
TIME						
TOTAL						

DINNER	DESCRIPTION	QTY	PROTEINS	VEGGIES	FRUITS & NUTS	FATS
TIME						
TOTAL						

SNACK	DESCRIPTION	QTY	PROTEINS	VEGGIES	FRUITS & NUTS	FATS
TIME						
TOTAL						

MEAL PLANNER

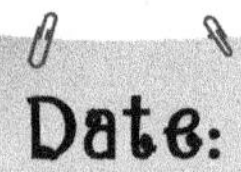

BREAK FAST

TIME

DESCRIPTION	QTY	PROTEINS	VEGGIES	FRUITS & NUTS	FATS
TOTAL					

LUNCH

TIME

DESCRIPTION	QTY	PROTEINS	VEGGIES	FRUITS & NUTS	FATS
TOTAL					

DINNER

TIME

DESCRIPTION	QTY	PROTEINS	VEGGIES	FRUITS & NUTS	FATS
TOTAL					

SNACK

TIME

DESCRIPTION	QTY	PROTEINS	VEGGIES	FRUITS & NUTS	FATS
TOTAL					

MEAL PLANNER

	DESCRIPTION	QTY	PROTEINS	VEGGIES	FRUITS & NUTS	FATS
BREAK FAST						
TIME						
TOTAL						

	DESCRIPTION	QTY	PROTEINS	VEGGIES	FRUITS & NUTS	FATS
LUNCH						
TIME						
TOTAL						

	DESCRIPTION	QTY	PROTEINS	VEGGIES	FRUITS & NUTS	FATS
DINNER						
TIME						
TOTAL						

	DESCRIPTION	QTY	PROTEINS	VEGGIES	FRUITS & NUTS	FATS
SNACK						
TIME						
TOTAL						

MEAL PLANNER

Date:

BREAK FAST

TIME

	DESCRIPTION	QTY	PROTEINS	VEGGIES	FRUITS & NUTS	FATS
TOTAL						

LUNCH

TIME

	DESCRIPTION	QTY	PROTEINS	VEGGIES	FRUITS & NUTS	FATS
TOTAL						

DINNER

TIME

	DESCRIPTION	QTY	PROTEINS	VEGGIES	FRUITS & NUTS	FATS
TOTAL						

SNACK

TIME

	DESCRIPTION	QTY	PROTEINS	VEGGIES	FRUITS & NUTS	FATS
TOTAL						

MEAL PLANNER

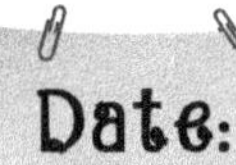

	DESCRIPTION	QTY	PROTEINS	VEGGIES	FRUITS & NUTS	FATS
BREAK FAST TIME						
TOTAL						

	DESCRIPTION	QTY	PROTEINS	VEGGIES	FRUITS & NUTS	FATS
LUNCH TIME						
TOTAL						

	DESCRIPTION	QTY	PROTEINS	VEGGIES	FRUITS & NUTS	FATS
DINNER TIME						
TOTAL						

	DESCRIPTION	QTY	PROTEINS	VEGGIES	FRUITS & NUTS	FATS
SNACK TIME						
TOTAL						

MEAL PLANNER

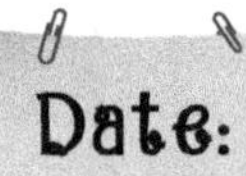

BREAK FAST

TIME

DESCRIPTION	QTY	PROTEINS	VEGGIES	FRUITS & NUTS	FATS
TOTAL					

LUNCH

TIME

DESCRIPTION	QTY	PROTEINS	VEGGIES	FRUITS & NUTS	FATS
TOTAL					

DINNER

TIME

DESCRIPTION	QTY	PROTEINS	VEGGIES	FRUITS & NUTS	FATS
TOTAL					

SNACK

TIME

DESCRIPTION	QTY	PROTEINS	VEGGIES	FRUITS & NUTS	FATS
TOTAL					

meal planner

Date:

BREAK FAST

TIME

DESCRIPTION	QTY	PROTEINS	VEGGIES	FRUITS & NUTS	FATS
TOTAL					

LUNCH

TIME

DESCRIPTION	QTY	PROTEINS	VEGGIES	FRUITS & NUTS	FATS
TOTAL					

DINNER

TIME

DESCRIPTION	QTY	PROTEINS	VEGGIES	FRUITS & NUTS	FATS
TOTAL					

SNACK

TIME

DESCRIPTION	QTY	PROTEINS	VEGGIES	FRUITS & NUTS	FATS
TOTAL					

MEAL PLANNER

Date:

	DESCRIPTION	QTY	PROTEINS	VEGGIES	FRUITS & NUTS	FATS
BREAK FAST						
TIME						
TOTAL						

	DESCRIPTION	QTY	PROTEINS	VEGGIES	FRUITS & NUTS	FATS
LUNCH						
TIME						
TOTAL						

	DESCRIPTION	QTY	PROTEINS	VEGGIES	FRUITS & NUTS	FATS
DINNER						
TIME						
TOTAL						

	DESCRIPTION	QTY	PROTEINS	VEGGIES	FRUITS & NUTS	FATS
SNACK						
TIME						
TOTAL						

MEAL PLANNER

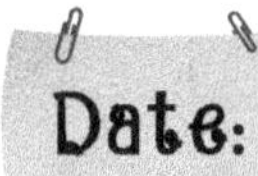

Date:

BREAK FAST

TIME

DESCRIPTION	QTY	PROTEINS	VEGGIES	FRUITS & NUTS	FATS
TOTAL					

LUNCH

TIME

DESCRIPTION	QTY	PROTEINS	VEGGIES	FRUITS & NUTS	FATS
TOTAL					

DINNER

TIME

DESCRIPTION	QTY	PROTEINS	VEGGIES	FRUITS & NUTS	FATS
TOTAL					

SNACK

TIME

DESCRIPTION	QTY	PROTEINS	VEGGIES	FRUITS & NUTS	FATS
TOTAL					

MEAL PLANNER

	DESCRIPTION	QTY	PROTEINS	VEGGIES	FRUITS & NUTS	FATS
BREAK FAST TIME						
TOTAL						

	DESCRIPTION	QTY	PROTEINS	VEGGIES	FRUITS & NUTS	FATS
LUNCH TIME						
TOTAL						

	DESCRIPTION	QTY	PROTEINS	VEGGIES	FRUITS & NUTS	FATS
DINNER TIME						
TOTAL						

	DESCRIPTION	QTY	PROTEINS	VEGGIES	FRUITS & NUTS	FATS
SNACK TIME						
TOTAL						

MEaL PLaNNER

Date:

BREAK FAST

DESCRIPTION	QTY	PROTEINS	VEGGIES	FRUITS & NUTS	FATS

TIME

TOTAL

LUNCH

DESCRIPTION	QTY	PROTEINS	VEGGIES	FRUITS & NUTS	FATS

TIME

TOTAL

DINNER

DESCRIPTION	QTY	PROTEINS	VEGGIES	FRUITS & NUTS	FATS

TIME

TOTAL

SNACK

DESCRIPTION	QTY	PROTEINS	VEGGIES	FRUITS & NUTS	FATS

TIME

TOTAL

MEAL PLANNER

BREAK FAST

TIME

TOTAL

	DESCRIPTION	QTY	PROTEINS	VEGGIES	FRUITS & NUTS	FATS

LUNCH

TIME

TOTAL

	DESCRIPTION	QTY	PROTEINS	VEGGIES	FRUITS & NUTS	FATS

DINNER

TIME

TOTAL

	DESCRIPTION	QTY	PROTEINS	VEGGIES	FRUITS & NUTS	FATS

SNACK

TIME

TOTAL

	DESCRIPTION	QTY	PROTEINS	VEGGIES	FRUITS & NUTS	FATS

MEAL PLANNER

Date:

BREAK FAST

TIME

DESCRIPTION	QTY	PROTEINS	VEGGIES	FRUITS & NUTS	FATS
TOTAL					

LUNCH

TIME

DESCRIPTION	QTY	PROTEINS	VEGGIES	FRUITS & NUTS	FATS
TOTAL					

DINNER

TIME

DESCRIPTION	QTY	PROTEINS	VEGGIES	FRUITS & NUTS	FATS
TOTAL					

SNACK

TIME

DESCRIPTION	QTY	PROTEINS	VEGGIES	FRUITS & NUTS	FATS
TOTAL					

MEAL PLANNER

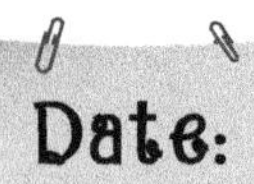

Date:

BREAK FAST

TIME

DESCRIPTION	QTY	PROTEINS	VEGGIES	FRUITS & NUTS	FATS
TOTAL					

LUNCH

TIME

DESCRIPTION	QTY	PROTEINS	VEGGIES	FRUITS & NUTS	FATS
TOTAL					

DINNER

TIME

DESCRIPTION	QTY	PROTEINS	VEGGIES	FRUITS & NUTS	FATS
TOTAL					

SNACK

TIME

DESCRIPTION	QTY	PROTEINS	VEGGIES	FRUITS & NUTS	FATS
TOTAL					

MEAL PLANNER

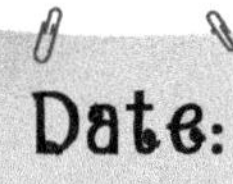

Date:

BREAK FAST

TIME

DESCRIPTION	QTY	PROTEINS	VEGGIES	FRUITS & NUTS	FATS
TOTAL					

LUNCH

TIME

DESCRIPTION	QTY	PROTEINS	VEGGIES	FRUITS & NUTS	FATS
TOTAL					

DINNER

TIME

DESCRIPTION	QTY	PROTEINS	VEGGIES	FRUITS & NUTS	FATS
TOTAL					

SNACK

TIME

DESCRIPTION	QTY	PROTEINS	VEGGIES	FRUITS & NUTS	FATS
TOTAL					

MEAL PLANNER

Date:

BREAK FAST	DESCRIPTION	QTY	PROTEINS	VEGGIES	FRUITS & NUTS	FATS
TIME						
TOTAL						

LUNCH	DESCRIPTION	QTY	PROTEINS	VEGGIES	FRUITS & NUTS	FATS
TIME						
TOTAL						

DINNER	DESCRIPTION	QTY	PROTEINS	VEGGIES	FRUITS & NUTS	FATS
TIME						
TOTAL						

SNACK	DESCRIPTION	QTY	PROTEINS	VEGGIES	FRUITS & NUTS	FATS
TIME						
TOTAL						

MEAL PLANNER

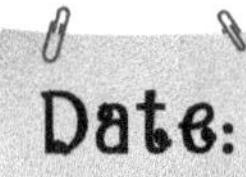

Date:

BREAK FAST

TIME

DESCRIPTION	QTY	PROTEINS	VEGGIES	FRUITS & NUTS	FATS
TOTAL					

LUNCH

TIME

DESCRIPTION	QTY	PROTEINS	VEGGIES	FRUITS & NUTS	FATS
TOTAL					

DINNER

TIME

DESCRIPTION	QTY	PROTEINS	VEGGIES	FRUITS & NUTS	FATS
TOTAL					

SNACK

TIME

DESCRIPTION	QTY	PROTEINS	VEGGIES	FRUITS & NUTS	FATS
TOTAL					

MEAL PLANNER

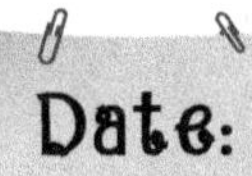

Date:

BREAK FAST

TIME

DESCRIPTION	QTY	PROTEINS	VEGGIES	FRUITS & NUTS	FATS
TOTAL					

LUNCH

TIME

DESCRIPTION	QTY	PROTEINS	VEGGIES	FRUITS & NUTS	FATS
TOTAL					

DINNER

TIME

DESCRIPTION	QTY	PROTEINS	VEGGIES	FRUITS & NUTS	FATS
TOTAL					

SNACK

TIME

DESCRIPTION	QTY	PROTEINS	VEGGIES	FRUITS & NUTS	FATS
TOTAL					

MEAL PLANNER

BREAK FAST

TIME

DESCRIPTION	QTY	PROTEINS	VEGGIES	FRUITS & NUTS	FATS
TOTAL					

LUNCH

TIME

DESCRIPTION	QTY	PROTEINS	VEGGIES	FRUITS & NUTS	FATS
TOTAL					

DINNER

TIME

DESCRIPTION	QTY	PROTEINS	VEGGIES	FRUITS & NUTS	FATS
TOTAL					

SNACK

TIME

DESCRIPTION	QTY	PROTEINS	VEGGIES	FRUITS & NUTS	FATS
TOTAL					

MEAL PLANNER

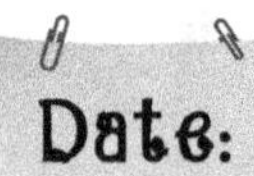

BREAK FAST

TIME

	DESCRIPTION	QTY	PROTEINS	VEGGIES	FRUITS & NUTS	FATS
TOTAL						

LUNCH

TIME

	DESCRIPTION	QTY	PROTEINS	VEGGIES	FRUITS & NUTS	FATS
TOTAL						

DINNER

TIME

	DESCRIPTION	QTY	PROTEINS	VEGGIES	FRUITS & NUTS	FATS
TOTAL						

SNACK

TIME

	DESCRIPTION	QTY	PROTEINS	VEGGIES	FRUITS & NUTS	FATS
TOTAL						

MEAL PLANNER

BREAK FAST

TIME

DESCRIPTION	QTY	PROTEINS	VEGGIES	FRUITS & NUTS	FATS
TOTAL					

LUNCH

TIME

DESCRIPTION	QTY	PROTEINS	VEGGIES	FRUITS & NUTS	FATS
TOTAL					

DINNER

TIME

DESCRIPTION	QTY	PROTEINS	VEGGIES	FRUITS & NUTS	FATS
TOTAL					

SNACK

TIME

DESCRIPTION	QTY	PROTEINS	VEGGIES	FRUITS & NUTS	FATS
TOTAL					

Meal Planner

Date:

BREAK FAST

TIME

DESCRIPTION	QTY	PROTEINS	VEGGIES	FRUITS & NUTS	FATS
TOTAL					

LUNCH

TIME

DESCRIPTION	QTY	PROTEINS	VEGGIES	FRUITS & NUTS	FATS
TOTAL					

DINNER

TIME

DESCRIPTION	QTY	PROTEINS	VEGGIES	FRUITS & NUTS	FATS
TOTAL					

SNACK

TIME

DESCRIPTION	QTY	PROTEINS	VEGGIES	FRUITS & NUTS	FATS
TOTAL					

MEAL PLANNER

Date:

BREAK FAST

TIME

DESCRIPTION	QTY	PROTEINS	VEGGIES	FRUITS & NUTS	FATS
TOTAL					

LUNCH

TIME

DESCRIPTION	QTY	PROTEINS	VEGGIES	FRUITS & NUTS	FATS
TOTAL					

DINNER

TIME

DESCRIPTION	QTY	PROTEINS	VEGGIES	FRUITS & NUTS	FATS
TOTAL					

SNACK

TIME

DESCRIPTION	QTY	PROTEINS	VEGGIES	FRUITS & NUTS	FATS
TOTAL					

meal Planner

 Date:

	DESCRIPTION	QTY	PROTEINS	VEGGIES	FRUITS & NUTS	FATS
BREAK FAST						
TIME						
TOTAL						

	DESCRIPTION	QTY	PROTEINS	VEGGIES	FRUITS & NUTS	FATS
LUNCH						
TIME						
TOTAL						

	DESCRIPTION	QTY	PROTEINS	VEGGIES	FRUITS & NUTS	FATS
DINNER						
TIME						
TOTAL						

	DESCRIPTION	QTY	PROTEINS	VEGGIES	FRUITS & NUTS	FATS
SNACK						
TIME						
TOTAL						

Meal Planner

Date:

BREAK FAST

TIME

DESCRIPTION	QTY	PROTEINS	VEGGIES	FRUITS & NUTS	FATS
TOTAL					

LUNCH

TIME

DESCRIPTION	QTY	PROTEINS	VEGGIES	FRUITS & NUTS	FATS
TOTAL					

DINNER

TIME

DESCRIPTION	QTY	PROTEINS	VEGGIES	FRUITS & NUTS	FATS
TOTAL					

SNACK

TIME

DESCRIPTION	QTY	PROTEINS	VEGGIES	FRUITS & NUTS	FATS
TOTAL					

meal planner

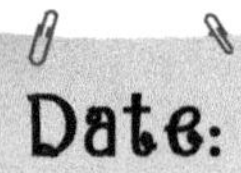

Date:

BREAK FAST

TIME

DESCRIPTION	QTY	PROTEINS	VEGGIES	FRUITS & NUTS	FATS
TOTAL					

LUNCH

TIME

DESCRIPTION	QTY	PROTEINS	VEGGIES	FRUITS & NUTS	FATS
TOTAL					

DINNER

TIME

DESCRIPTION	QTY	PROTEINS	VEGGIES	FRUITS & NUTS	FATS
TOTAL					

SNACK

TIME

DESCRIPTION	QTY	PROTEINS	VEGGIES	FRUITS & NUTS	FATS
TOTAL					

MEAL PLANNER

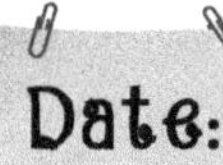

Date:

BREAKFAST

TIME ☐

DESCRIPTION	QTY	PROTEINS	VEGGIES	FRUITS & NUTS	FATS
TOTAL					

LUNCH

TIME ☐

DESCRIPTION	QTY	PROTEINS	VEGGIES	FRUITS & NUTS	FATS
TOTAL					

DINNER

TIME ☐

DESCRIPTION	QTY	PROTEINS	VEGGIES	FRUITS & NUTS	FATS
TOTAL					

SNACK

TIME ☐

DESCRIPTION	QTY	PROTEINS	VEGGIES	FRUITS & NUTS	FATS
TOTAL					

meal Planner

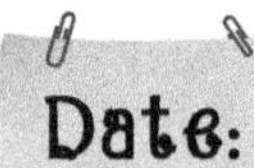

	DESCRIPTION	QTY	PROTEINS	VEGGIES	FRUITS & NUTS	FATS
BREAK FAST						
TIME						
TOTAL						

	DESCRIPTION	QTY	PROTEINS	VEGGIES	FRUITS & NUTS	FATS
LUNCH						
TIME						
TOTAL						

	DESCRIPTION	QTY	PROTEINS	VEGGIES	FRUITS & NUTS	FATS
DINNER						
TIME						
TOTAL						

	DESCRIPTION	QTY	PROTEINS	VEGGIES	FRUITS & NUTS	FATS
SNACK						
TIME						
TOTAL						

MEAL PLANNER

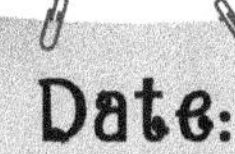

Date:

BREAK FAST

TIME

DESCRIPTION	QTY	PROTEINS	VEGGIES	FRUITS & NUTS	FATS
TOTAL					

LUNCH

TIME

DESCRIPTION	QTY	PROTEINS	VEGGIES	FRUITS & NUTS	FATS
TOTAL					

DINNER

TIME

DESCRIPTION	QTY	PROTEINS	VEGGIES	FRUITS & NUTS	FATS
TOTAL					

SNACK

TIME

DESCRIPTION	QTY	PROTEINS	VEGGIES	FRUITS & NUTS	FATS
TOTAL					

meat planner

Date:

	DESCRIPTION	QTY	PROTEINS	VEGGIES	FRUITS & NUTS	FATS
BREAK FAST						
TIME						
TOTAL						

	DESCRIPTION	QTY	PROTEINS	VEGGIES	FRUITS & NUTS	FATS
LUNCH						
TIME						
TOTAL						

	DESCRIPTION	QTY	PROTEINS	VEGGIES	FRUITS & NUTS	FATS
DINNER						
TIME						
TOTAL						

	DESCRIPTION	QTY	PROTEINS	VEGGIES	FRUITS & NUTS	FATS
SNACK						
TIME						
TOTAL						

meal planner

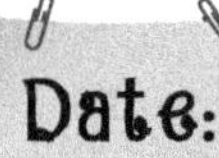

Date:

BREAK FAST

TIME

DESCRIPTION	QTY	PROTEINS	VEGGIES	FRUITS & NUTS	FATS
TOTAL					

LUNCH

TIME

DESCRIPTION	QTY	PROTEINS	VEGGIES	FRUITS & NUTS	FATS
TOTAL					

DINNER

TIME

DESCRIPTION	QTY	PROTEINS	VEGGIES	FRUITS & NUTS	FATS
TOTAL					

SNACK

TIME

DESCRIPTION	QTY	PROTEINS	VEGGIES	FRUITS & NUTS	FATS
TOTAL					

meal Planner

Date:

BREAK FAST

TIME

DESCRIPTION	QTY	PROTEINS	VEGGIES	FRUITS & NUTS	FATS
TOTAL					

LUNCH

TIME

DESCRIPTION	QTY	PROTEINS	VEGGIES	FRUITS & NUTS	FATS
TOTAL					

DINNER

TIME

DESCRIPTION	QTY	PROTEINS	VEGGIES	FRUITS & NUTS	FATS
TOTAL					

SNACK

TIME

DESCRIPTION	QTY	PROTEINS	VEGGIES	FRUITS & NUTS	FATS
TOTAL					

MEAL PLANNER

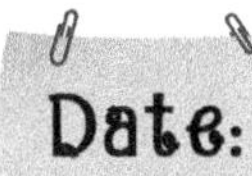

Date:

BREAK FAST

TIME

DESCRIPTION	QTY	PROTEINS	VEGGIES	FRUITS & NUTS	FATS
TOTAL					

LUNCH

TIME

DESCRIPTION	QTY	PROTEINS	VEGGIES	FRUITS & NUTS	FATS
TOTAL					

DINNER

TIME

DESCRIPTION	QTY	PROTEINS	VEGGIES	FRUITS & NUTS	FATS
TOTAL					

SNACK

TIME

DESCRIPTION	QTY	PROTEINS	VEGGIES	FRUITS & NUTS	FATS
TOTAL					

MEAL PLANNER

Date:

	DESCRIPTION	QTY	PROTEINS	VEGGIES	FRUITS & NUTS	FATS
BREAK FAST TIME						
TOTAL						

	DESCRIPTION	QTY	PROTEINS	VEGGIES	FRUITS & NUTS	FATS
LUNCH TIME						
TOTAL						

	DESCRIPTION	QTY	PROTEINS	VEGGIES	FRUITS & NUTS	FATS
DINNER TIME						
TOTAL						

	DESCRIPTION	QTY	PROTEINS	VEGGIES	FRUITS & NUTS	FATS
SNACK TIME						
TOTAL						

MEAL PLANNER

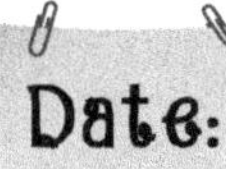

Date:

BREAK FAST

TIME

DESCRIPTION	QTY	PROTEINS	VEGGIES	FRUITS & NUTS	FATS
TOTAL					

LUNCH

TIME

DESCRIPTION	QTY	PROTEINS	VEGGIES	FRUITS & NUTS	FATS
TOTAL					

DINNER

TIME

DESCRIPTION	QTY	PROTEINS	VEGGIES	FRUITS & NUTS	FATS
TOTAL					

SNACK

TIME

DESCRIPTION	QTY	PROTEINS	VEGGIES	FRUITS & NUTS	FATS
TOTAL					

www.ingramcontent.com/pod-product-compliance
Lightning Source LLC
Chambersburg PA
CBHW081311250726
48662CB00008B/2515